PENGUIN YOUNG READERS LICENSES
An Imprint of Penguin Random House LLC

✳ Smithsonian

This trademark is owned by the Smithsonian Institution and
is registered in the U.S. Patent and Trademark Office.

Smithsonian Enterprises:
Christopher Liedel, President
Carol LeBlanc, Senior Vice President, Education and Consumer Products
Brigid Ferraro, Vice President, Education and Consumer Products
Ellen Nanney, Licensing Manager
Kealy Gordon, Product Development Manager

Stephen Binns, Writer, Smithsonian Center for Learning and Digital Access

Text copyright © 2017 by Penguin Random House LLC and Smithsonian Institution.
All rights reserved. Published by Penguin Young Readers Licenses, an imprint of
Penguin Random House LLC, 345 Hudson Street, New York, New York 10014.
Manufactured in China.

Library of Congress Cataloging-in-Publication Data is available.

ISBN 9780515157741   10 9 8 7 6 5 4 3 2 1

CONTENTS

USA ALL THE WAY!

These fascinating facts about the 50 states will leave you in a state of amazement, a state of wonder, and maybe even a state of shock!

Read all about stuff that will make you say, "NO WAY!" ... but "WAY!" Everything in this book is 100% true.

USA! Let's go!

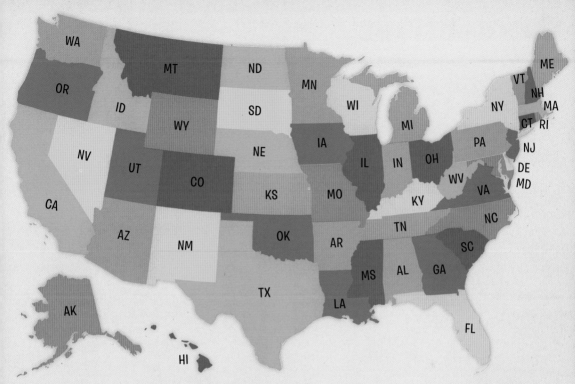

AL	=	Alabama	IN	=	Indiana	NE	=	Nebraska	SC	=	South Carolina
AK	=	Alaska	IA	=	Iowa	NV	=	Nevada	SD	=	South Dakota
AZ	=	Arizona	KS	=	Kansas	NH	=	New Hampshire	TN	=	Tennessee
AR	=	Arkansas	KY	=	Kentucky	NJ	=	New Jersey	TX	=	Texas
CA	=	California	LA	=	Louisiana	NM	=	New Mexico	UT	=	Utah
CO	=	Colorado	ME	=	Maine	NY	=	New York	VT	=	Vermont
CT	=	Connecticut	MD	=	Maryland	NC	=	North Carolina	VA	=	Virginia
DE	=	Delaware	MA	=	Massachusetts	ND	=	North Dakota	WA	=	Washington
FL	=	Florida	MI	=	Michigan	OH	=	Ohio	WV	=	West Virginia
GA	=	Georgia	MN	=	Minnesota	OK	=	Oklahoma	WI	=	Wisconsin
HI	=	Hawaii	MS	=	Mississippi	OR	=	Oregon	WY	=	Wyoming
ID	=	Idaho	MO	=	Missouri	PA	=	Pennsylvania			
IL	=	Illinois	MT	=	Montana	RI	=	Rhode Island			

Connecticut

Connecticut is clock country! After the American Revolution, Eli Terry pioneered the mass production of clocks in this state.

STATE INSECT:
PRAYING MANTIS

THIS BUG CAN TURN ITS HEAD 180 DEGREES!

LOUIS' LUNCH IN NEW HAVEN HAS BEEN
SERVING HAMBURGERS WITH NO KETCHUP
OR MUSTARD SINCE 1900—AND THAT'S
THE WAY YOU HAVE TO EAT THEM THERE!

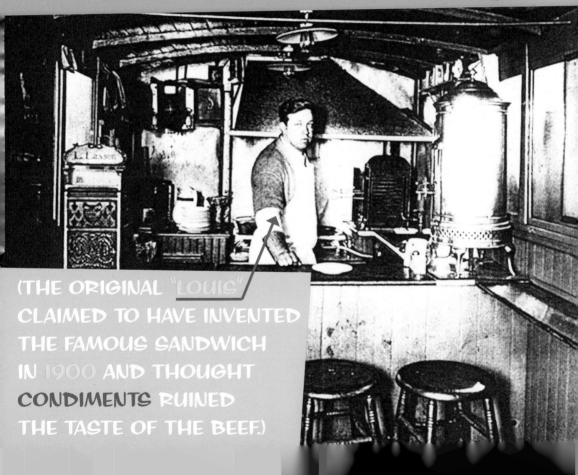

(THE ORIGINAL "LOUIS"
CLAIMED TO HAVE INVENTED
THE FAMOUS SANDWICH
IN 1900 AND THOUGHT
CONDIMENTS RUINED
THE TASTE OF THE BEEF.)

Connecticut-born author <u>Harriet Beecher Stowe</u> helped change public opinion about slavery with her novel <u>*Uncle Tom's Cabin*</u> (1851).

UNCLE TOM'S CABIN

UNCLE TOM & EVA.

Thank Connecticut for ...

anesthesia, first used by a Connecticut dentist in 1844 to remove his own tooth.

Copyright by R. Chickering 1901

speed limits, first passed here in 1901: only 12 miles per hour!

CONNECTICUT COMES FROM THE MOHEGAN LANGUAGE AND MEANS "LONG RIVER PLACE."

Maine

Maine is the only state with a one-syllable name.

Watch out for **moose!** There are 76,000 of them in this state.

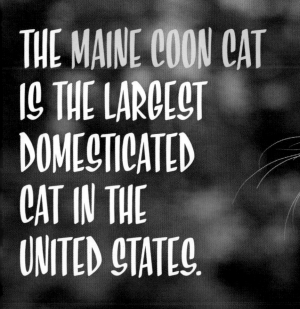

THE MAINE COON CAT IS THE LARGEST DOMESTICATED CAT IN THE UNITED STATES.

Up until 2003, Strong, Maine, was known as the "Toothpick Capital of the World." The rise of dental floss caused the toothpick factories to close.

Follow up your lobster dinner with some **wild blueberry pie.** Maine grows more **wild blueberries** than any place in the world.

THANK MAINE FOR . . .

NIGHTMARES. STEPHEN KING, AUTHOR OF SPOOKY STORIES, LIVES AND WRITES IN THIS STATE.

Massachusetts

BAY STATE

Massachusetts has a special holiday: Patriot's Day, the third Monday in April. It celebrates the first battles of the American Revolution.

YOU COULD HAVE BREWED 18.5 MILLION CUPS OF TEA WITH ALL THE TEA DUMPED DURING THE BOSTON TEA PARTY PROTEST.

Massachusetts native Clara Barton was a Civil War nurse who founded the American Red Cross.

U.S.

Signatures are called "John Hancocks" after the Massachusetts-born president of the Second Continental Congress. His signature is the biggest on the Declaration of Independence.

Salem, Massachusetts, is called "Witch City." In 1692-93, 20 people were executed there for witchcraft—their trials were later declared unlawful.

Thank Massachusetts for . . .

volleyball, called "Mintonette" when it was invented here in 1895.

underground travel. The first US subway system was built in Boston in 1897.

Boston cream pie. It's the official state dessert.

New Hampshire

GRANITE STATE

Granite from New Hampshire was used to build the Library of Congress in Washington, DC.

It's also what the "Old Man of the Mountain" was made of. (This famous rocky outcrop collapsed in 2003.)

THE STATE MOTTO IS

"LIVE FREE OR DIE"

WRITTEN BY GENERAL JOHN STARK,
NEW HAMPSHIRE'S
REVOLUTIONARY WAR HERO.

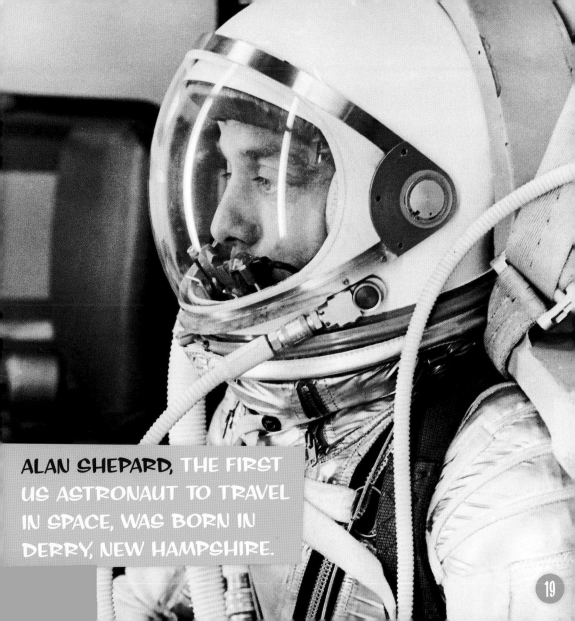

ALAN SHEPARD, THE FIRST US ASTRONAUT TO TRAVEL IN SPACE, WAS BORN IN DERRY, NEW HAMPSHIRE.

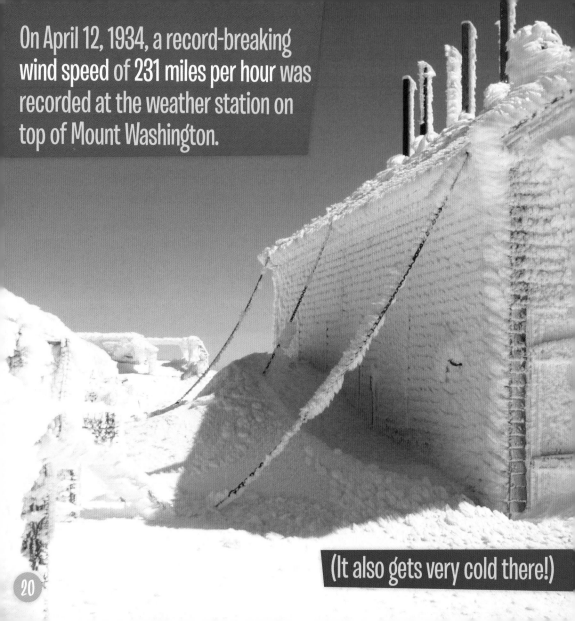

On April 12, 1934, a record-breaking wind speed of 231 miles per hour was recorded at the weather station on top of Mount Washington.

(It also gets very cold there!)

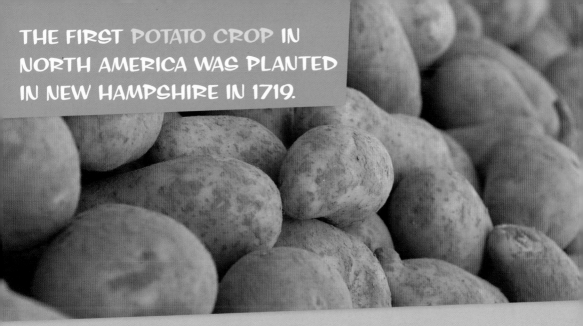

THE FIRST POTATO CROP IN NORTH AMERICA WAS PLANTED IN NEW HAMPSHIRE IN 1719.

The first US presidential primary is held here every four years.

Thank New Hampshire for...

road trips. The first planned, scenic US car route was the Mount Washington Auto Road.

New Jersey

GARDEN STATE

NEW JERSEY WAS ONCE TWO-THIRDS FARMLAND. WHEN "GARDEN STATE" BECAME ITS OFFICIAL NICKNAME IN 1954, LESS THAN 3% OF THE STATE'S INHABITANTS WORKED IN AGRICULTURE.

New Jersey astronaut Buzz Aldrin walked on the moon. His name was the inspiration for *Toy Story*'s Buzz Lightyear!

Some people think the map of New Jersey looks like a guy's head.

22

THE HOLLAND TUNNEL RUNS UNDER THE HUDSON RIVER AND CONNECTS NEW YORK AND NEW JERSEY; 34 MILLION VEHICLES ROLL THROUGH THE TUNNEL EVERY YEAR; 84 ENORMOUS FANS CHANGE THE AIR EVERY 90 SECONDS TO CLEAR OUT THE CAR FUMES.

Most Crowded State: More people are packed in per square mile in New Jersey than in any other state.

24

IN 1909, A TROLLEY CAR IN HADDON HEIGHTS, NEW JERSEY, WAS SAID TO HAVE BEEN ATTACKED BY A CREATURE WITH A GOAT'S BODY AND BAT WINGS: THE JERSEY DEVIL.

New Jersey holds the US record for most stolen cars every year.

THANK NEW JERSEY FOR . . .

RECORD PLAYERS, LIGHTBULBS, AND MOVIES, ALL INVENTED HERE BY THOMAS EDISON IN THE 1800s.

New York

MANHATTAN

QUEENS

BROOKLYN

OF MANNAHATTA !

New York City has 722 miles of subway track. Laid end to end, they'd stretch from Manhattan to South Carolina!

NEW YORK IS THE MOST POPULOUS CITY IN THE COUNTRY. A BABY IS BORN THERE EVERY 4.4 MINUTES!

Lightning strikes the Empire State Building (ESB) an average of 23 times a year.

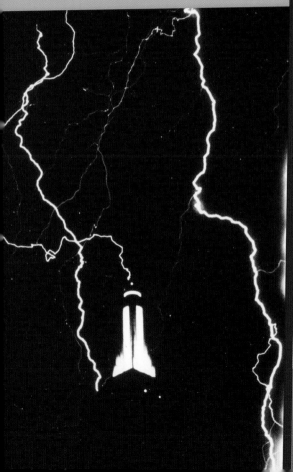

THE ESB HOLDS SO MANY BUSINESSES THAT IT HAS ITS OWN ZIP CODE!

27

Alexander Hamilton founded the *New York Post* newspaper in 1801. It's the longest-running daily paper in the United States.

Adirondack Park is bigger than Grand Canyon, Yellowstone, Everglades, and Glacier National Parks combined.

In a famous story by Washington Irving, Rip Van Winkle meets some mysterious men bowling in the Catskill Mountains, drinks their strange brew, and falls asleep for decades.

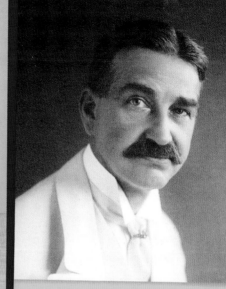

Follow the yellow brick *sidewalk*? Chittenango, New York, laid colored bricks to honor homeboy **L. Frank Baum**, author of *The Wonderful Wizard of Oz*.

THANK NEW YORK . . .

THE NEXT TIME YOU USE THE BATHROOM. **TOILET PAPER WAS** INVENTED HERE!

29

Pennsylvania

KEYSTONE STATE

A **keystone** is the stone in the center of an arch that keeps it from falling down. Pennsylvania, the place where the Declaration of Independence and US Constitution were signed, was the "keystone" of the 13 colonies.

THE CONTINENTAL CONGRESS MET IN PHILADELPHIA AND VOTED FOR INDEPENDENCE. THE DECLARATION OF INDEPENDENCE WAS DATED JULY 4, 1776, BUT IT WASN'T SIGNED UNTIL AUGUST 2.

ROUND THE WORLD WITH NELLIE BLY.

CUT OUT THIS GAME, PLACE IT ON A TABLE OR PASTE IT ON CARDBOARD AND PLAY ACCORDING TO SIMPLE DIRECTIONS BELOW.

Pennsylvania-born reporter Nellie Bly read Jules Verne's *Around the World in 80 Days* and decided to try to beat that time. She did it in 72 days—in 1889.

George Washington and Betsy Ross attended the same church in Philadelphia. She sewed his shirt cuffs for him.

BENJAMIN FRANKLIN WAS BORN IN BOSTON BUT MOVED TO PHILADELPHIA, WHERE HE BECAME A FAMOUS PRINTER, INVENTOR, SCIENTIST, AND FOUNDING FATHER.

Tech Savvy: PA was the first state to put its URL on license plates.

Legend says that groundhog Punxsutawney Phil has been predicting the weather since 1887, which would make him 130 years old. (Non-legendary groundhogs live about eight years.)

THANK PENNSYLVANIA FOR . . .

ZOOS! PHILADELPHIA OPENED THE NATION'S FIRST ZOO IN 1874.

SNACKS! THIS STATE IS THE LEADING PRODUCER OF POTATO CHIPS, PRETZELS, ICE CREAM, AND CANDY.

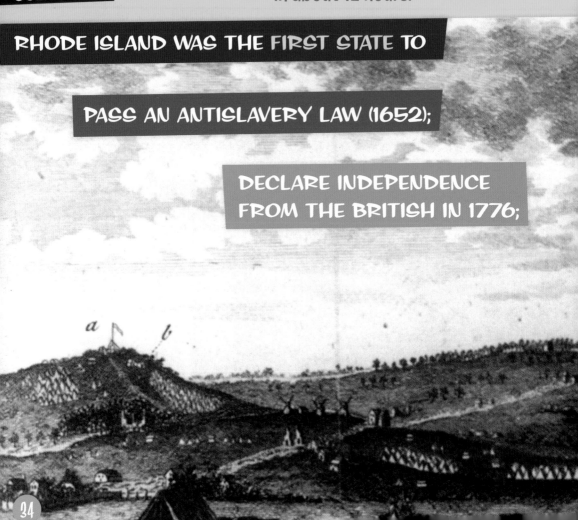

Rhode Island

OCEAN STATE

You could **walk** across Rhode Island in about 12 hours.

RHODE ISLAND WAS THE FIRST STATE TO

PASS AN ANTISLAVERY LAW (1652);

DECLARE INDEPENDENCE FROM THE BRITISH IN 1776;

The smallest US state has the longest official name: the State of Rhode Island and Providence Plantations.

RAISE A REGIMENT OF AFRICAN AMERICAN SOLDIERS. THEY FOUGHT THE BRITISH IN THE BATTLE OF RHODE ISLAND IN 1778.

DINERS! THE FIRST ONE WAS A HORSE-DRAWN LUNCH CART THAT OPENED IN PROVIDENCE, RHODE ISLAND, IN 1872.

Sideburns! Civil War general (who later became governor) Ambrose Burnside started the trend, and "burnsides" later became "sideburns."

37

Vermont

Vermont comes from *montagne verte*, French for "green mountain."

VERMONT'S CANDIDATES FOR GOVERNOR AND LIEUTENANT GOVERNOR IN 1886 EACH ONLY HAD ONE ARM. THEIR CAMPAIGN SLOGAN: "TWO GOOD ARMS BETWEEN THE TWO OF US."

Safest state: Vermont has the lowest rate of violent crime in the United States.

BILLBOARD ADVERTISING IS NOT ALLOWED IN VERMONT (OR IN ALASKA, HAWAII, OR MAINE, EITHER).

IN 1982, VERMONT PASSED A STATE RESOLUTION TO PROTECT "CHAMP," A **LAKE MONSTER** SAID TO LIVE IN LAKE CHAMPLAIN.

SUGAR MAPLE

THANK VERMONT FOR . . .

TASTIER PANCAKES! THIS STATE PRODUCES 500,000 GALLONS OF MAPLE SYRUP A YEAR, MORE THAN ANY OTHER STATE.

41

Alabama

YELLOWHAMMER STATE

CIVIL WAR SOLDIERS FROM ALABAMA WORE UNIFORMS TRIMMED IN YELLOW. THEY WERE CALLED "YELLOWHAMMERS," AFTER A WOODPECKER WITH YELLOW FEATHERS ON ITS WINGS AND TAIL.

Rosa Parks's refusal to give up her seat on a segregated public bus in Montgomery, Alabama, in 1955—and the bus boycott that followed—sparked the Civil Rights Movement.

Vulcan, the world's largest cast iron statue, weighs 50 tons and was made of Alabama iron.

Magnolia Springs, Alabama, has the only all-water US mail delivery route that operates all year long.

Alabama's state quarter is the first to feature braille, in honor of Alabama-born Helen Keller.

Alabama was the first state to set up 911 calls (1968);

declare Christmas a legal holiday (1836);

run an electric trolley (1886).

The Saturn V rocket that put humans on the moon (1969) was built in Huntsville.

45

Arkansas

NATURAL STATE

ARKANSAS BECAME THE "NATURAL STATE" IN 1995 TO CELEBRATE THE BEAUTIFUL SCENERY THERE. (BEFORE THAT, IT WAS THE "LAND OF OPPORTUNITY.")

WELCOME TO
Arkansas
THE NATURAL STATE®
BUCKLE UP FOR SAFETY

SPANISH EXPLORER HERNANDO DE SOTO VISITED ARKANSAS IN 1541—79 YEARS BEFORE THE PILGRIMS LANDED IN MASSACHUSETTS.

You say "Ar-Kansas," I say "Arkan-saw." In 1881 a law passed and settled the pronunciation on "Arkan-saw."

ARKANSAS HAS THE ONLY ACTIVE DIAMOND MINE IN THE UNITED STATES.

Ozark National Forest takes up more than 1 million acres in northern Arkansas.

Hattie Caraway of Arkansas was the first woman elected to the US Senate (1932); in 1943 she became the first woman to preside over the Senate.

THANK ARKANSAS FOR . . .

movies with sound, perfected by Arkansas native Freeman Owens;

fried pickles, created in 1963 by the owner of a drive-in movie theater;

rice. No US state grows more rice than Arkansas.

Delaware

FIRST STATE

Delaware was the "First State" to ratify the US Constitution.

THE FIRST **LOG CABIN** IN THE US WAS BUILT HERE BY SWEDISH SETTLERS, PROBABLY AROUND 1638.

The state fossil is belemnite, a squid-like creature that went extinct when the dinosaurs did.

The 330-mile Delaware River is the longest river east of the Mississippi. It was named after the colonial governor of Virginia, Lord De La Warr. The state was then named after the river.

THE TOWN OF DELMAR IS HALF IN MARYLAND AND HALF IN DELAWARE.

You'll find more horseshoe crabs in Delaware Bay than anywhere else in the world. These "living fossils" were around long before the time of the dinosaurs.

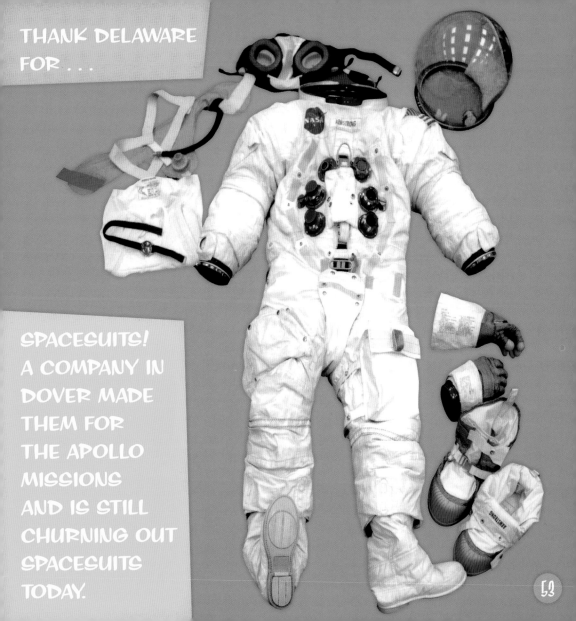

THANK DELAWARE FOR . . .

SPACESUITS! A COMPANY IN DOVER MADE THEM FOR THE APOLLO MISSIONS AND IS STILL CHURNING OUT SPACESUITS TODAY.

Florida

The rockets that shot Americans into orbit and then landed men on the moon all launched from Cape Canaveral, Florida.

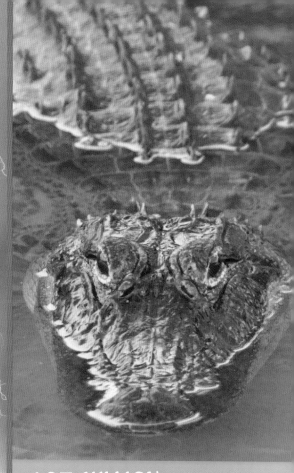

Shocking fact! Lightning strikes Florida more than any other state in the nation: 1.2 million times a year!

1.25 MILLION ALLIGATORS LIVE IN FLORIDA. THAT'S MORE THAN TWICE THE POPULATION OF MIAMI!

Venice, Florida, is the "Shark Tooth Capital of the World," where people flock to hunt for fossilized shark teeth.

THERE ARE ONLY TWO NATURALLY ROUND LAKES IN THE WHOLE WORLD, AND ONE OF THEM IS IN DEFUNIAK SPRINGS, FLORIDA.

THANK FLORIDA FOR . . .

YOUR REFRIGERATOR!
A FLORIDIAN PATENTED AN
ICE-MAKING MACHINE IN →
1851. (MAKES SENSE WHEN
YOU THINK ABOUT IT!)

FOOTBALL PLAYERS!
IN 2015, MORE NFL
PLAYERS CAME FROM
FLORIDA THAN ANY
OTHER STATE.

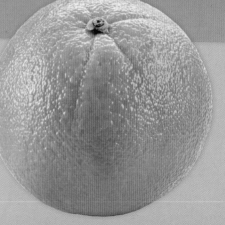

ORANGES! THE FIRST
ORANGES IN AMERICA
WERE PLANTED IN
THE 1500s IN FLORIDA,
POSSIBLY BY EXPLORER
PONCE DE LEÓN.

Georgia

PEACH STATE

GEORGIA WAS NAMED AFTER ENGLAND'S KING GEORGE II. (HIS IDEA!)

Despite the legends, you won't find buried treasure on Georgia's **Blackbeard Island**.

But you will find lots of migratory seabirds at the wildlife refuge there.

59

GEORGIA MIGHT BE CALLED THE "PEACH STATE," BUT THESE DAYS CALIFORNIA PRODUCES 20 TIMES MORE PEACHES.

Welcome We're glad Georgia's on your mind

More than 100 million passengers pass through Hartsfield-Jackson Atlanta International Airport each year, making it the busiest in the world.

In Gainesville, Chicken Capital of the World, it's against the law to eat fried chicken with a fork. (But you won't get arrested if you do!)

THE WORLD'S SWEETEST ONION. IT CAN ONLY BE GROWN IN 13 COUNTIES IN GEORGIA.

GIRL SCOUTS. THE GROUP WAS FOUNDED BY JULIETTE GORDON LOW IN SAVANNAH IN 1912.

Kentucky

BLUEGRASS STATE

Shawnee, Mohawk, Delaware, Wyandot, or Catawba words may have been the source of the name Kentucky; many of them mean "meadowland" or "prairie."

MORE THAN HALF OF THE AMERICANS KILLED IN THE WAR OF 1812 WERE FROM KENTUCKY.

Why is bluegrass blue? The plants' buds have a bluish-purple hue.

KENTUCKY USED TO BE PART OF VIRGINIA. THEY BROKE UP IN 1792. (THE APPALACHIAN MOUNTAINS BETWEEN THE STATES HAD A LOT TO DO WITH IT.)

The federal government stores gold worth nearly $200 billion in Fort Knox, Kentucky.

Abraham Lincoln | Jefferson Davis

Abraham Lincoln, the leader of the Union in the Civil War, and Jefferson Davis, the leader of the Confederacy, were both born in Kentucky.

AT 400 MILES, KENTUCKY'S MAMMOTH CAVE IS THE LONGEST CAVE STRUCTURE IN THE WORLD.

Head to Cumberland Falls in Kentucky on a clear, full-moon night, and you might see a moonbow, a lunar rainbow.

THANK KENTUCKY FOR . . .

BIRTHDAY SERENADES. "HAPPY BIRTHDAY TO YOU" WAS WRITTEN BY TWO KENTUCKY SISTERS.

Louisiana

PELICAN STATE

The brown pelican, Louisiana's state bird, dives from the air into the water to catch fish.

THE <u>LOUISIANA PURCHASE</u> OF 1803 DOUBLED THE SIZE OF THE UNITED STATES OVERNIGHT, CREATING PARTS OR ALL OF WHAT BECAME 15 STATES.

The Louisiana state capitol building is the tallest in the country.

LOUISIANA WAS THE FIRST STATE TO:

HOST AN OPERA PERFORMANCE (1796);

OPEN A MOVIE THEATER WITH SEATS AND TICKETS: VITASCOPE HALL, NEW ORLEANS (1896).

67

1881 The Prophetic Mirror-of-the-Sea 2017

More than 1,000 floats fill the streets of New Orleans in **Mardi Gras** parades every year.

THE LONGEST BRIDGE ENTIRELY OVER WATER IS LOUISIANA'S 24-MILE LAKE PONTCHARTRAIN CAUSEWAY. IT'S HELD UP BY 9,000 CONCRETE PILINGS.

THANK LOUISIANA FOR . . .

JAZZ! THIS FORM OF MUSIC WAS CREATED WHEN EUROPEAN SOUNDS MET THE RHYTHMS OF AFRICA.

Maryland

OLD LINE STATE

MARYLAND'S SOLDIERS IN THE AMERICAN REVOLUTION WERE DUBBED THE "OLD LINE" BECAUSE THEY WERE AMONG THE FIRST TO JOIN THE WAR.

Lawyer Francis Scott Key watched the British bombard an American fort in Baltimore, Maryland, during the War of 1812. He was inspired to write "The Star-Spangled Banner," which became the US national anthem.

The first **stagecoach** route ran from Baltimore to Philadelphia, Pennsylvania.

Babe Ruth, the "King of Swat," grew up in Baltimore, where he was once sent to reform school for bad behavior.

The famous **wild ponies** on Assateague Island are thought to be descendants of animals that survived a Spanish shipwreck in the 1500s.

YOU'LL FIND MORE HOT SPRINGS HERE THAN IN ANY OTHER STATE.

THANK MARYLAND FOR . . .

STAYING DRY! THE FIRST UMBRELLAS PRODUCED IN AMERICA WERE MADE IN BALTIMORE IN 1828.

Mississippi

Mississippi means "great river." The name is a French interpretation of an Ojibwe word. The Mississippi River flows along ten states.

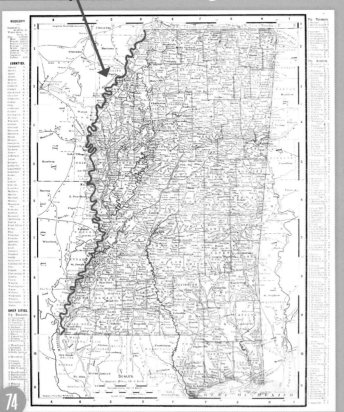

74

MISSISSIPPI STEAMBOATS WERE KNOWN FOR THEIR SPEED AT TRAVELING THE RIVER: 5 MPH!

Memorial Day began on May 30, 1868, when women in Columbus, Mississippi, put flowers on the graves of both Union and Confederate soldiers.

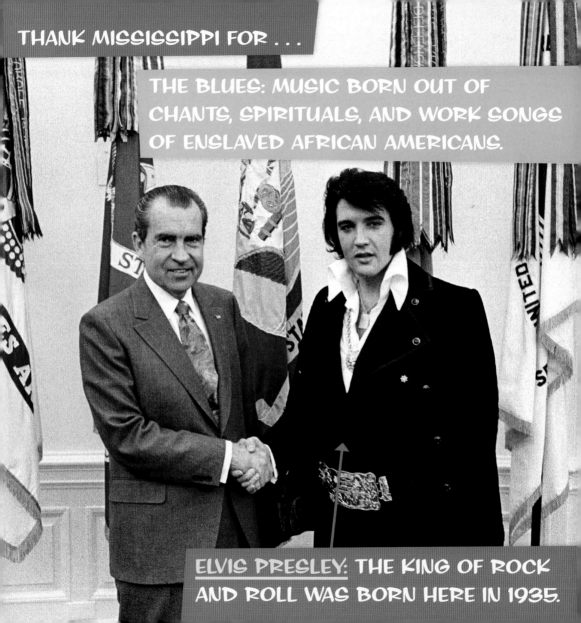

THANK MISSISSIPPI FOR . . .

THE BLUES: MUSIC BORN OUT OF CHANTS, SPIRITUALS, AND WORK SONGS OF ENSLAVED AFRICAN AMERICANS.

ELVIS PRESLEY: THE KING OF ROCK AND ROLL WAS BORN HERE IN 1935.

North Carolina

Colonists in this state were called "tar heels" because they boiled tar, which was made from the state's many pine trees and used to coat ships.

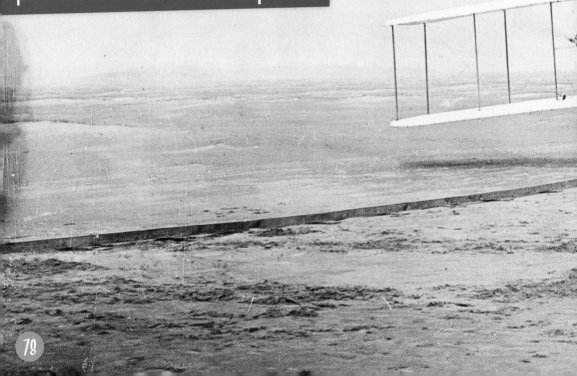

North Carolina license plates read "First in Flight" because the Wright brothers launched their first successful airplane flight in 1903 at Kitty Hawk.

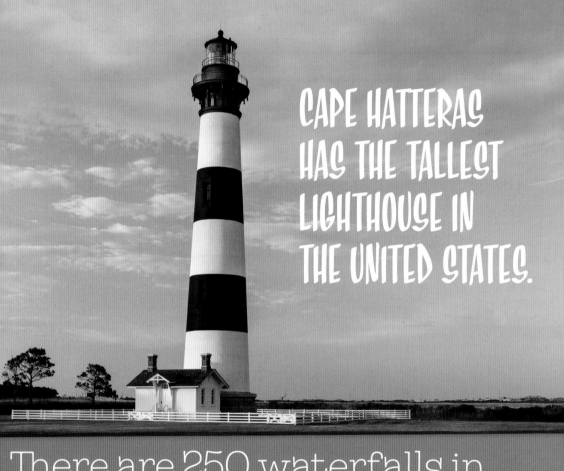

CAPE HATTERAS HAS THE TALLEST LIGHTHOUSE IN THE UNITED STATES.

There are 250 waterfalls in North Carolina's Transylvania County—but no vampires!

North Carolina and South Carolina are the only US states where you can see a Venus flytrap eat an insect in the wild (if that's something you want to see!).

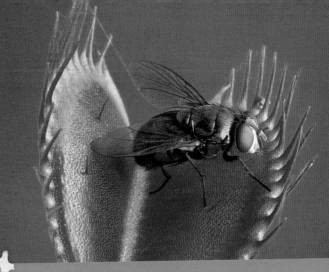

Virginia Dare, the first English child born in America, came into the world in North Carolina in 1587 (although back then it was still called Virginia).

THANK NORTH CAROLINA FOR . . .

SWEET POTATO FRIES! MORE SWEET POTATOES ARE GROWN HERE THAN IN ANY OTHER STATE.

South Carolina

THE BRITISH SPLIT CAROLINA INTO TWO COLONIES, NORTH AND SOUTH, IN 1729.

During the American Revolution, British cannonballs bounced off the palmetto-tree logs used to build a fort on Sullivan's Island, hence the state nickname and flag.

The Carolina Reaper,
the hottest chili pepper in the world,
is 312 times hotter than a jalapeño!

SOUTH CAROLINA WAS THE FIRST STATE TO:

have a golf course, which opened in 1786;

leave the Union to form the Confederacy (1860).

THANK SOUTH CAROLINA FOR . . .

SWEET TEA, FIRST SERVED HERE IN 1890.

Tennessee

VOLUNTEER STATE

Memphis, Tennessee, is named after the ancient city of Memphis in Egypt.

When the United States went to war with Mexico in 1846, each state was asked for 2,800 volunteer soldiers—3,000 Tennesseans answered the call.

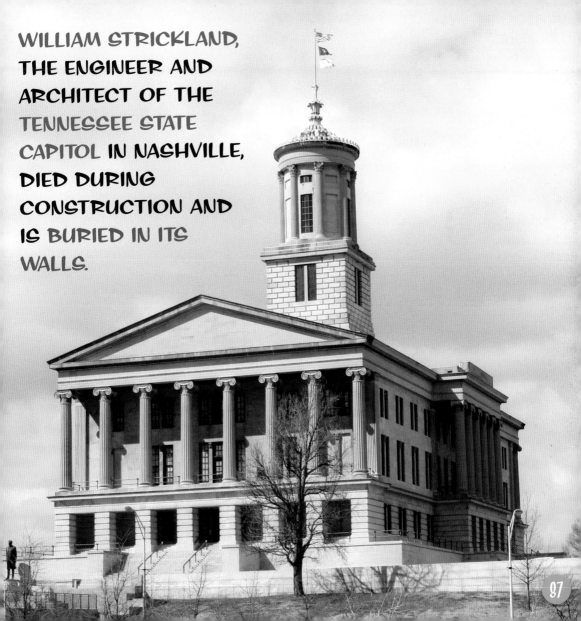

WILLIAM STRICKLAND, THE ENGINEER AND ARCHITECT OF THE TENNESSEE STATE CAPITOL IN NASHVILLE, DIED DURING CONSTRUCTION AND IS BURIED IN ITS WALLS.

87

Like amphibians? The Great Smoky Mountains National Park is home to 30 different species of salamanders, the most diverse population in the world.

DENTIST WILLIAM MORRISON OF NASHVILLE INVENTED A MACHINE THAT MADE COTTON CANDY IN 1897.

SINCE 1840, COLUMBIA, TENNESSEE, HAS CELEBRATED MULE DAY EVERY SPRING. THE CELEBRATIONS INCLUDE THE CROWNING OF A MULE QUEEN.

Three large earthquakes hit Tennessee between 1811 and 1812. They could be felt as far away as New York!

Thank Tennessee for . . .

road rescues. The tow truck was invented in Chattanooga in 1916.

country music on the radio. The Grand Ole Opry in Nashville started broadcasting nationally in 1925.

Virginia

OLD DOMINION STATE

More presidents have been born in Virginia than in any other state.

Washington

Jefferson

Madison

Monroe

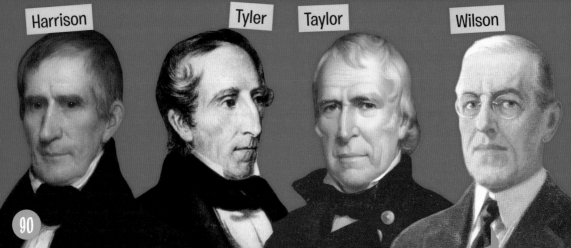

Harrison

Tyler

Taylor

Wilson

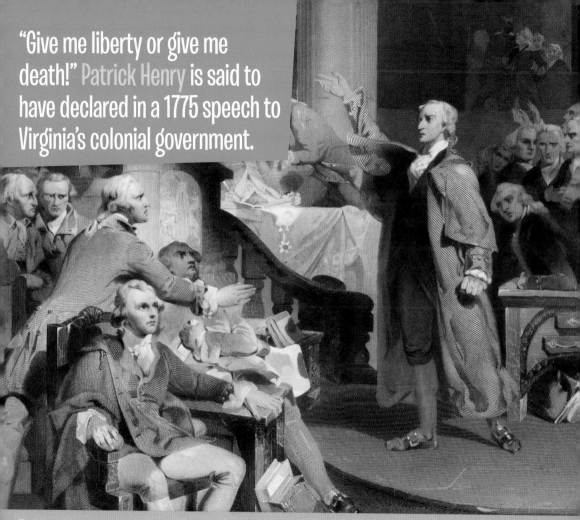

"Give me liberty or give me death!" Patrick Henry is said to have declared in a 1775 speech to Virginia's colonial government.

Virginia was the first and oldest colony in the Americas under the "dominion" or control of the rulers of England.

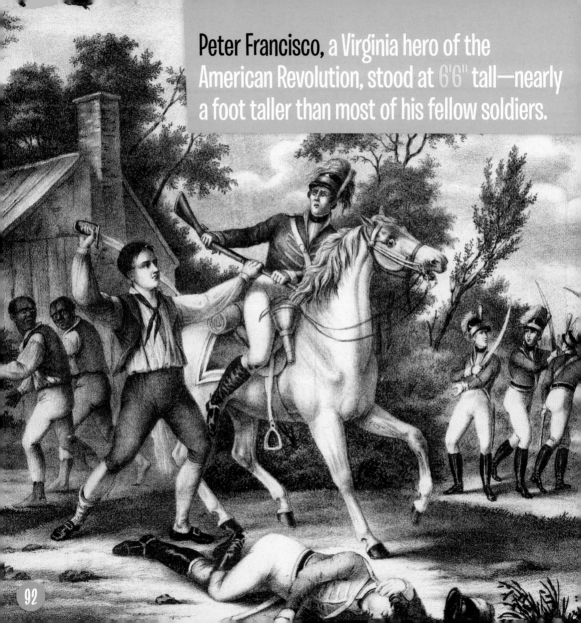

Peter Francisco, a Virginia hero of the American Revolution, stood at 6'6" tall—nearly a foot taller than most of his fellow soldiers.

MORE THAN HALF OF ALL CIVIL WAR BATTLES WERE FOUGHT IN VIRGINIA.

A Virginian starting school before Labor Day? No way! A 1986 state law says school has to start after the holiday—courtesy of the state's tourism industry! (Though some districts get waivers.)

THANK VIRGINIA FOR . . .

WEB SURFING. MOST OF THE COUNTRY'S INTERNET TRAFFIC GOES THROUGH DATA CENTERS IN VIRGINIA.

West Virginia

West Virginia is one of the chief US exporters of coal.

WEST VIRGINIA BECAME ITS OWN STATE AFTER VIRGINIA **SECEDED FROM THE UNION.** (LIKE KENTUCKY, THE APPALACHIAN MOUNTAINS HAD A LOT TO DO WITH THE BREAKUP!)

West Virginia's New River is one of the oldest in the world. Some of the rocks found in its bed are more than one billion years old!

New River Gorge Bridge is closed for a day in October so people can **bungee** off it.

GRANDPARENTS DAY! WEST VIRGINIAN MARIAN McQUADE HAD THE IDEA FOR THE HOLIDAY, AND IN 1978 PRESIDENT JIMMY CARTER MADE IT OFFICIAL. IT'S CELEBRATED EVERY YEAR ON THE FIRST SUNDAY AFTER LABOR DAY.

97

Iowa

HAWKEYE STATE

More than 200 sacred earthen mounds built by Woodland Indians are preserved in Effigy Mounds National Monument in Iowa. Some are in the shape of animals.

IOWA IS THE ONLY STATE NAME THAT STARTS WITH TWO VOWELS.

The state nickname comes from a character named Hawkeye in James Fenimore Cooper's novel *The Last of the Mohicans*—which takes place in New York.

Burlington's Snake Alley competes with Lombard Street in San Francisco for the title of world's most crooked street.

The Red Delicious apple was first grown in 1872 in an orchard in Peru, Iowa.

Iowa native Buffalo Bill Cody rode for the Pony Express at age 14 before becoming a Civil War hero.

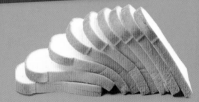

SLICED BREAD. THE FIRST AUTOMATIC BREAD-SLICING MACHINE WAS INVENTED IN DAVENPORT.

BREAKFAST, LUNCH, AND DINNER. THE AVERAGE IOWA FAMILY FARM GROWS ENOUGH FOOD TO FEED 279 PEOPLE.

Only two buildings survived the Great Chicago Fire of 1871: a water tower and a water-pumping station.

THE FIRST SKYSCRAPER WAS BUILT IN CHICAGO IN 1885. IT HAD A FIREPROOF STEEL FRAME.

THE CHICAGO RIVER IS DYED GREEN EVERY ST. PATRICK'S DAY (MARCH 17).

More than 26 million people visited the World's Columbian Exposition in Chicago in 1893, which included marvels like the first Ferris wheel.

THANK ILLINOIS FOR . . .

YOUR CELL PHONE. THE FIRST WERE DEVELOPED HERE IN THE 1970S.

THE DISHWASHER, INVENTED BY JOSEPHINE COCHRANE IN 1893 BECAUSE SHE WAS TIRED OF WASHING DISHES BY HAND.

THE ICE CREAM SUNDAE, INVENTED IN EVANSTON (OR SO SAY FOLKS IN ILLINOIS).

Indiana

HOOSIER STATE

THE NICKNAME "HOOSIER" MIGHT COME FROM HOOSHER, A WORD USED TO DESCRIBE THE BRAVERY AND SELF-RELIANCE OF THE STATE'S EARLY PIONEERS. NOBODY KNOWS FOR CERTAIN.

More than 2,000 people escaped slavery by passing through Fountain City, Indiana, a stop on the Underground Railroad. Levi Coffin's house was a major stop.

More spectators can fit in the Indianapolis Motor Speedway than in any other sporting facility. NO WAY...

WAY! There are more than 250,000 permanent seats.

THE WINNER OF THE INDY 500 DRINKS A BOTTLE OF BUTTERMILK AFTER THE RACE— IN HOMAGE TO THE FIRST GUY WHO DID THAT BACK IN 1936.

Santa Claus, Indiana, gets more than 500,000 letters to Santa each year. One of the first theme parks in the country opened here: Santa Claus Land (now called Holiday World).

THANK INDIANA FOR . . .

CLEAN CLOTHES. WILLIAM BLACKSTONE INVENTED THE WASHING MACHINE FOR THE HOME HERE IN 1874.

Kansas

SUNFLOWER STATE

Kansas produces more wheat than any other state—about 235 million bushels a year.

1 bushel = 45 boxes of cereal!

No WAY! Late 1800s: Kansas lawmakers label the sunflower a "noxious weed." WAY! 1903: It becomes the state flower.

Want to stand in the exact center of the continental United States?

Head to Smith County, Kansas.

When Dorothy in *The Wizard of Oz* movie clicks her heels and says, "There's no place like home," she's talking about Kansas. (In the book, her shoes were silver.)

Several states claim to have the "World's Largest Ball of Twine"—like this one in Cawker City, Kansas.

You'll find more wild grouse in Kansas than in any other state. This bird is nicknamed the "prairie chicken."

THANK KANSAS FOR . . .

BIRTHDAY BALLOONS! HELIUM WAS DISCOVERED IN A KANSAS WELL IN 1906, KICKING OFF THE AMERICAN HELIUM INDUSTRY.

Michigan
GREAT LAKES STATE

The Great Lakes contain more than 80% of North America's surface freshwater supply.

Michigan borders 4 of the 5 Great Lakes.

No point in Michigan is farther than 6 miles from a lake or river.

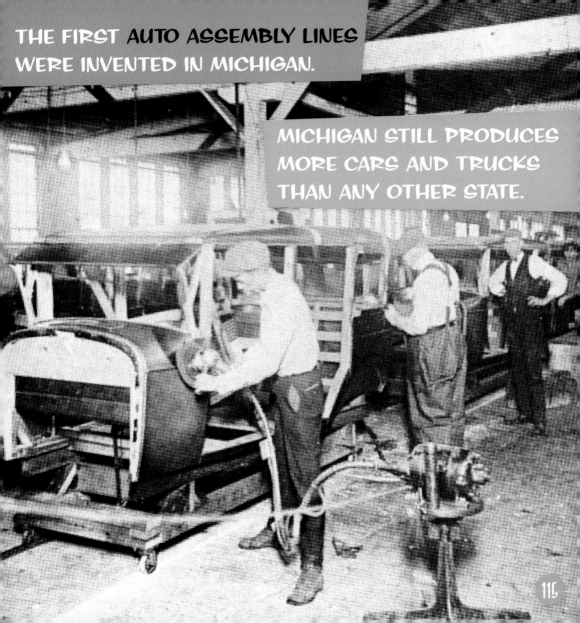

THE FIRST AUTO ASSEMBLY LINES
WERE INVENTED IN MICHIGAN.

MICHIGAN STILL PRODUCES
MORE CARS AND TRUCKS
THAN ANY OTHER STATE.

Henry Ford's workers could produce a Model T in 93 minutes, thanks to conveyor belts on the assembly lines.

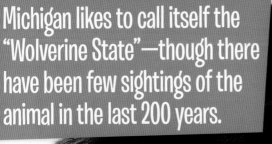

Michigan likes to call itself the "Wolverine State"—though there have been few sightings of the animal in the last 200 years.

Thank Michigan for . . .

safe travels. The first yellow lines separating road lanes, and the first four-way traffic light, were created in Michigan.

baby food. The soft stuff was first canned here in 1928.

Minnesota

MINNESOTA'S OFFICIAL MOTTO IS *L'ETOILE DU NORD*, WHICH MEANS "STAR OF THE NORTH." MINNESOTANS BELIEVE THEIR STATE IS A SHINING STAR IN THE NORTHERN PART OF THE COUNTRY.

Minnesota is also known as the "Land of 10,000 Lakes"—but there are **11,842 lakes** here.

There are enough recreational boats in this state for 1 in every 6 people.

Several cities claim to be the birthplace of legendary folk hero **Paul Bunyan,** including Akeley and Bemidji, Minnesota.

HAPPY BIRTHDAY, BIG FELLA!

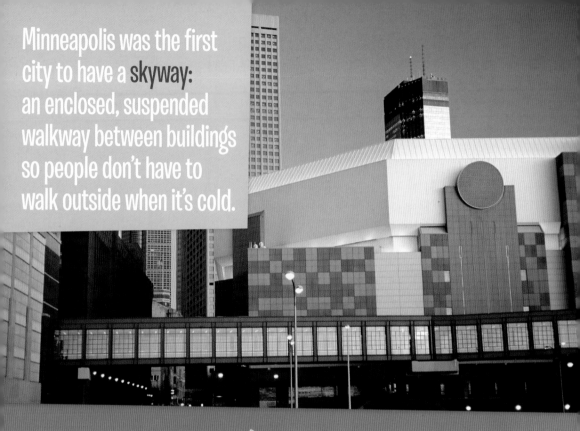

Minneapolis was the first city to have a **skyway:** an enclosed, suspended walkway between buildings so people don't have to walk outside when it's cold.

MINNESOTA'S MALL OF AMERICA IS BIG ENOUGH TO FIT 32 BOEING 747s INSIDE.

Some people believe that **Vikings** explored Minnesota more than 1,000 years ago, but most scholars say they're wrong. Don't tell that to the Minnesota Vikings football team!

THANK MINNESOTA FOR . . .

MICROWAVE POPCORN, INVENTED HERE IN 1984.

MEDICAL MIRACLES. THE FIRST SUCCESSFUL OPEN-HEART SURGERY WAS PERFORMED IN THIS STATE.

Missouri

SHOW-ME STATE

Missouri's 630-foot Gateway Arch is the state's tallest monument.

Legend says that the state nickname came from a Missouri congressman who once said that fancy words didn't impress him: "I'm from Missouri. You have to show me."

Charles Lindbergh made a historic flight across the Atlantic in a plane called *The Spirit of St. Louis,* named in honor of the Missouri businessmen who paid for the trip.

MISSOURI-BORN SCIENTIST GEORGE WASHINGTON CARVER DISCOVERED MORE THAN 100 USES FOR THE PEANUT, INCLUDING FUEL.

Thank Missouri for . . .

kindergarten! Missourian Susan Elizabeth Blow opened the first American public kindergarten in 1873.

iced tea and ice cream cones, invented at the St. Louis World's Fair in 1804 (according to Missouri folks!).

Nebraska

Nebraska comes from an Oto word meaning "flat water."

THE OMAHA, PAWNEE, OTOE, SANTEE SIOUX, WINNEBAGO, PONCA, IOWA, SAC, AND FOX WERE ALL LIVING IN NEBRASKA WHEN EUROPEAN SETTLERS ARRIVED.

The 2015 men's cornhusking state champ picked and husked 461 pounds of corn in 30 minutes.

SUSAN LA FLESCHE PICOTTE, OF THE NEBRASKA OMAHA TRIBE, WAS THE FIRST AMERICAN INDIAN WOMAN TO BECOME A DOCTOR.

ONE OF NEBRASKA'S MOST FAMOUS RESIDENTS HAS BEEN DEAD FOR 20,000 YEARS. "ARCHIE" IS THE WORLD'S LARGEST MAMMOTH SKELETON.

Hungry for a *runza?*

Nebraska is the only place you'll find this meat-and-cabbage-stuffed pastry.

Thank Nebraska for…

Arbor Day! This tree-planting holiday started here in 1872.

If you dig the earth…
plant trees!

North Dakota

PEACE GARDEN STATE

TO GOD IN HIS GLORY,

WE TWO NATIONS
DEDICATE THIS GARDEN,
AND PLEDGE OURSELVES
THAT AS LONG AS MEN
SHALL LIVE, WE WILL
NOT TAKE UP ARMS
AGAINST ONE ANOTHER

THE INTERNATIONAL PEACE GARDEN ON THE BORDER OF THE UNITED STATES AND CANADA REPRESENTS PEACE BETWEEN THE TWO COUNTRIES.

WHY ARE THERE TWO DAKOTAS?

THE DAKOTA TERRITORY WAS SPLIT IN 1889: NORTH DAKOTA BECAME THE 39TH AND SOUTH DAKOTA THE 40TH STATE.

More sunflowers are grown in North Dakota than in any other state. A sunflower is made up of 1,000 to 2,000 smaller flowers.

Visitors to North Dakota's annual French Fry Feed eat more than two tons of the crispy taters each year.

THANK NORTH DAKOTA FOR . . .

HONEY! THIS STATE PRODUCES MORE THAN ANY OTHER (WITH THE HELP OF BEES, OF COURSE).

Ohio
BUCKEYE STATE

The Buckeye is Ohio's state tree. Its nuts look like the eye of a male deer: a buck.

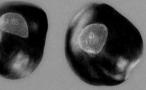

Ohio comes from the Iroquois word for "great (or good) river."

OHIO'S CUYAHOGA RIVER HAS CAUGHT FIRE 13 TIMES BECAUSE OF POLLUTION.

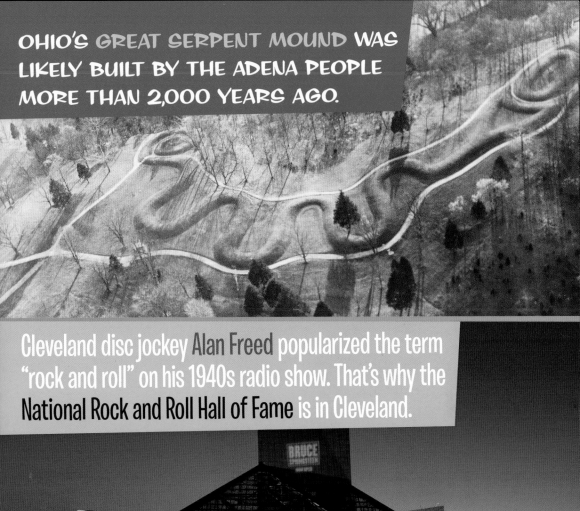

OHIO'S GREAT SERPENT MOUND WAS LIKELY BUILT BY THE ADENA PEOPLE MORE THAN 2,000 YEARS AGO.

Cleveland disc jockey Alan Freed popularized the term "rock and roll" on his 1940s radio show. That's why the National Rock and Roll Hall of Fame is in Cleveland.

SEVEN PRESIDENTS WERE BORN IN OHIO, INCLUDING ULYSSES S. GRANT.

Astronaut John Glenn, first American in orbit, was born in Ohio, too.

Neil Armstrong, first person to step on the moon, took his own first steps in Ohio.

OHIO WAS THE FIRST STATE TO . . .

HAVE A PRO BASEBALL TEAM, THE CINCINNATI RED STOCKINGS.

ISSUE A SPEEDING TICKET (1904). THE DRIVER WAS DOING 12 MPH.

South Dakota

MOUNT RUSHMORE STATE

Most of Mount Rushmore was carved using dynamite.

The heads are about 6 stories high and have 20-foot noses—except for Washington, whose nose is 21 feet! (Pays to be the *first* president.)

SOUTH DAKOTA HAS MORE SHORELINE THAN FLORIDA, THANKS TO THE MISSOURI RIVER AND LOTS OF LAKES.

The decorations on the outside of the Corn Palace in Mitchell, South Dakota, are made of corn, other grains, and grasses.

South Dakota's Wind Cave is the first cave national park. It is famous for its rare boxwork patterns formed by calcite crystals.

OGLALA LAKOTA CHIEF CRAZY HORSE AND HUNKPAPA LAKOTA CHIEF SITTING BULL, LEADERS DURING THE AMERICAN INDIAN WARS OF THE 1870s, WERE BOTH BORN IN SOUTH DAKOTA.

THE **BLACK-FOOTED FERRET,** ONE OF NORTH AMERICA'S MOST ENDANGERED SPECIES, HAS BEEN REINTRODUCED IN SOUTH DAKOTA.

Competitors flock to Clark, South Dakota, to enter the mashed-potato wrestling matches at the annual Potato Days Festival.

Wisconsin

Four states have an upside-down White House as a tourist attraction, including Wisconsin.

Wisconsin is called the Badger State not after the furry burrowing animal—but after the lead miners who "burrowed" into the hills to make their homes.

THE WORST FOREST FIRE IN AMERICAN HISTORY BLAZED THROUGH WISCONSIN IN 1871, KILLING MORE THAN 1,200 PEOPLE AND DESTROYING BILLIONS OF TREES.

Wisconsin produces more cheese than any other state; some inhabitants call themselves "Cheeseheads."

Wisconsin produced 3.3 billion gallons of milk in 2015—enough for 52.8 billion bowls of cereal.

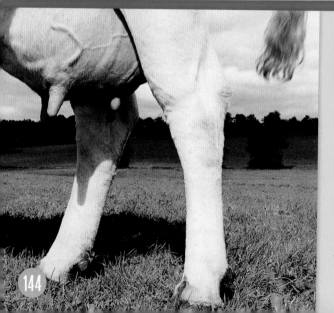

IT TAKES 340-350 SQUIRTS FROM A COW'S UDDER TO GET ONE GALLON OF MILK.

Green Bay, Wisconsin, is known as the "Toilet Paper Capital of the World" because the first splinter-free toilet paper was produced there. (They have a football team, too. Go, Packers!)

THANK WISCONSIN FOR . . .

MAGIC. HARRY HOUDINI GREW UP IN APPLETON, WISCONSIN.

CLASSIC BOOKS. LAURA INGALLS WILDER WAS BORN IN A LOG CABIN NEAR PEPIN, WISCONSIN, AND WROTE ABOUT IT IN LITTLE HOUSE IN THE BIG WOODS. THIS IS A REPLICA OF THE HOUSE.

Arizona

GRAND CANYON STATE

Arizona was originally part of New Mexico.

NEVADA

UTAH

Reno-Sparks Colony
Carson Colony
Stewart Community
Washoe Ranches
Dresslerville Colony
Woodfords Community

Fallon Colony
Fallon

Walker River

Yomba

Yerington
Yerington Colony

Washoe Tribe of Nevada
and California - Allotments

California

Goshute

Uintah
and Ouray

White

Ely Colony

Duckwater

Uintah and Ouray
Trust Land

Kanosh

Koosharem

Indian Peaks

Cedar City

Shivwitz

Las Vegas
Colony

Moapa
River

Kaibab

Hopi - Moencopi

Havasupai

Hualapai

San Juan
Southern Paiute

Hopi

Hualapai
Big Sandy

Fort Mojave

ARIZONA

Chemehuevi

Colorado River

Camp
Verde

Hopi Ranches

Yavapai

Fort McDowell

Salt River

Gila River

Tonto
Apache

Fort Apache

San Carlos

Gila Bend

Fort Yuma (Quechan)

Cocopah Maricopa
(Ak-Chin)

Tohono O'odham

Pascua Yaqui

San Xavier

Mexico

Owens River

Salinas River

Kern River

Kern River

Colorado River

Colorado River

Green River

San Juan River

Little Colorado River

Gila River

Gila River

There is more <u>Indian
tribal land</u> in Arizona
than in any other state.

ORAIBI IS A HOPI VILLAGE IN ARIZONA THAT'S BEEN AROUND FOR ALMOST A THOUSAND YEARS. IT'S THE OLDEST CONTINUOUSLY INHABITED SETTLEMENT IN THE US.

Arizona doesn't observe Daylight Saving Time, but the Navajo Nation in the northeast corner of the state does.

Arizona's population exploded in the 1920s, when residential air conditioning was introduced.

A **Saguaro cactus** can live for 200 years. If you cut one down in Arizona, you could serve up to 25 years in jail.

THANK ARIZONA FOR . . .

AMERICA'S GREATEST NATURAL WONDER. THE GRAND CANYON IS 277 MILES LONG, 18 MILES WIDE, AND A MILE DEEP.

New Mexico

LAND OF ENCHANTMENT

"Land of Enchantment" appeared on New Mexico license plates in 1941 to advertise the state's beauty. It became the official nickname in 1999.

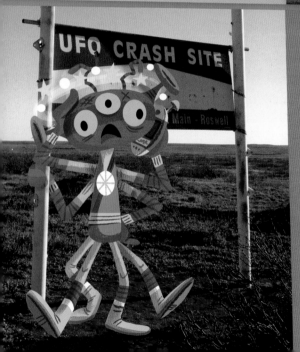

In 1947, a rancher in Roswell, New Mexico, discovered strange debris on his land. To this day, many people believe he found a crashed flying saucer.

Snow in the desert? **NO WAY...**
This is **White Sands National Monument,** the largest gypsum dune field in the world.

The first **atomic bomb** was tested in Alamogordo, New Mexico, in 1945. The explosion sent a huge mushroom cloud into the sky, and the desert sand fused into glass for 800 yards around the blast site!

New Mexico has the lowest water-to-land ratio of any state.

Sheep and cattle outnumber people in New Mexico.

Heads up! Every night 250,000 bats flap out of Carlsbad Caverns.

THANK NEW MEXICO FOR . . .

FIRE SAFETY! SMOKEY BEAR, THE MASCOT OF AN AD CAMPAIGN, WAS CREATED IN 1944. SIX YEARS LATER, A CUB WAS RESCUED FROM A NEW MEXICO FOREST FIRE. IT MOVED TO THE SMITHSONIAN'S NATIONAL ZOO AND BECAME FAMOUS AS THE "LIVING SYMBOL" OF SMOKEY.

FIRE DANGER
HIGH
TODAY!
PREVENT FOREST FIRES

Oklahoma

SOONER STATE

Oklahoma City was hit with 147 tornadoes between 1890 and 2011.

NO WAY...

WAY! In 1974, five tornadoes hit in just one day!

On March 2, 1889, the government opened up land in Oklahoma to settlers. Some sneaked in earlier than the deadline and were dubbed "Sooners."

OKLAHOMA HAS MORE ARTIFICIAL LAKES THAN ANY OTHER STATE.

Beaver, Oklahoma, is the Cow Chip Throwing Capital of the World. (A cow chip isn't a cookie—it's dried cow poop!)

MORE THAN 1 MILLION OKLAHOMANS MIGRATED TO CALIFORNIA DURING THE 1930s DUST BOWL.

Thank Oklahoma for ...

roadside attractions! Oklahoma native Cyrus Avery had the idea to build Route 66 to connect Chicago and Los Angeles.

Businesses along this highway built big sculptures to attract travelers—like Oklahoma's 80-foot-long Giant Blue Whale.

Texas

Texas comes from a Caddo word meaning friends or allies. The state motto? Friendship!

Texas was originally part of Mexico. It fought a war for independence, including the famous battle of the Alamo in 1835. Jim Bowie, Davy Crockett, and about 200 soldiers held off thousands of General Santa Ana's troops for 13 days before being overrun and killed.

THE JOHNSON SPACE CENTER IN HOUSTON HAS BEEN NASA'S MISSION CONTROL CENTER SINCE 1961.

THE FIRST WORD SPOKEN ON THE MOON? "HOUSTON."

HOUSTON'S **ASTRODOME** WAS THE FIRST DOME-SHAPED STADIUM.

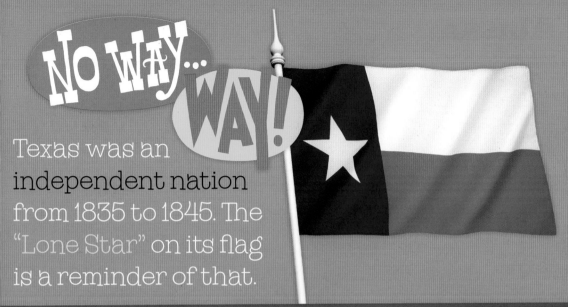

NO WAY... WAY!

Texas was an independent nation from 1835 to 1845. The "Lone Star" on its flag is a reminder of that.

THANK TEXAS FOR . . .

HAMBURGERS. THE STATE IS HOME TO ABOUT 16 MILLION CATTLE—MORE THAN ANY OTHER STATE.

Alaska

LAST FRONTIER

Alaska comes from an Inuit word meaning "great land."

ALASKA IS THE BIGGEST STATE. IT'S MORE THAN TWICE AS BIG AS TEXAS . . . BUT THERE ARE ONLY 1.2 ALASKANS PER SQUARE MILE!

The United States purchased Alaska from Russia for 2¢ per acre. Now that's a bargain!

A 13-YEAR-OLD BOY IN SEWARD DESIGNED THE
ALASKA STATE FLAG IN 1927. STELLAR JOB!

At 20,308 feet, Alaska's **Denali** is the **highest peak** in North America (and about 9,000 feet shorter than Mount Everest).

Salmon are born in freshwater, live most of their lives in salt water, and then return to freshwater to spawn.

THANK ALASKA FOR . . .

SEAFOOD! MOST OF THE COUNTRY'S SALMON, CRAB, HALIBUT, AND HERRING COME FROM THE WATERS IN AND AROUND ALASKA.

California

The hottest precisely recorded temperature on Earth was taken in California's Death Valley: 134 degrees (57 C).

California has the largest tree in the world (by volume), the General Sherman sequoia, and the oldest tree, a bristlecone that's more than 5,000 years old. (Shhh! The Forest Service is keeping its location a secret for the bristlecone's safety.)

MINERS SHOUTED "EUREKA!" WHEN THEY STRUCK GOLD IN THE CALIFORNIA GOLD RUSH OF 1849, HENCE THE STATE MOTTO.

This state's name was inspired by a 16th-century Spanish novel about an island paradise, *Califia*, inhabited by women warriors. (Spanish explorers originally thought they'd discovered an island.)

Thank California for . . .

fruit salad! One half of all the fruit grown in the United States is planted here.

your favorite movies! Moviemaking began on the east coast, but moved to Los Angeles. Sunshine nearly every day meant it was easier to film there.

HOLLYWOOD

Colorado

CENTENNIAL STATE

Colorado comes from the Spanish word for "colored red."

It's named after the Colorado River, which can appear red due to the silt from its riverbed.

COLORADO'S ROYAL GORGE BRIDGE SPANS A GORGE 1,000 FEET DEEP, MAKING THIS THE HIGHEST BRIDGE IN THE UNITED STATES.

The Pikes Peak Cog Railway is the highest train line in the United States. Train cars use gear, or cog, wheels and a special track to make the steep trip to the top of the 14,115-foot mountain.

Katherine Lee Bates was so inspired by the view from Pikes Peak that she wrote "America the Beautiful."

COLORADO HAS
THE WORLD'S
LARGEST
POPULATION
OF WILD ELK:
300,000.

Colorado became a state in 1876, 100 years after the nation was formed. A 100-year anniversary is called a centennial so ... *bam!* Nickname.

THANK COLORADO FOR ...

ROOT BEER FLOATS! FRANK J. WISNER OF CRIPPLE CREEK SUPPOSEDLY GAZED UPON MOONLIT, SNOW-CAPPED COW MOUNTAIN AND THOUGHT IT LOOKED LIKE ICE CREAM FLOATING IN SODA.

Hawaii

The Hawaiian language has 12 letters.

Aloha is a Hawaiian word that means love or peace. It is also now commonly used for "hello" and "good-bye."

BARACK OBAMA IS THE ONLY PRESIDENT BORN IN HAWAII.

THIS STATE IS A GROUP OF <u>VOLCANIC ISLANDS</u> WITH ITS OWN TIME ZONE: HAWAIIAN STANDARD TIME.

HAWAII WAS THE LAST STATE ADMITTED TO THE UNION (AUGUST 21, 1959).

All eight US battleships moored in **Pearl Harbor** were either sunk or destroyed when the Japanese attacked on December 7, 1941.

The United States then entered World War II.

THE VOLCANO MAUNA KEA IS THE TALLEST MOUNTAIN IN THE WORLD—IF YOU MEASURE IT FROM BELOW SEA LEVEL.

KILAUEA IS ONE OF THE MOST ACTIVE VOLCANOES IN THE WORLD. IT HAS BEEN ERUPTING CONSTANTLY SINCE 1983.

THANK HAWAII FOR . . .

COFFEE! IT'S NOT THE ONLY PLACE IN THE WORLD THAT GROWS IT, BUT IT'S THE ONLY US STATE THAT DOES.

Idaho

GEM STATE

More than 240 different minerals have been found in the "Gem State."

Scenic **IDAHO**

551 UTR

FAMOUS POTATOES

024275

15

U TRLR

178

Idaho grows more potatoes than any other state. Its license plate takes note.

IDAHO HAS 3,000 MILES OF RIVERS, MORE THAN ANY OTHER STATE.

THE FIRST CITY LIT BY ATOMIC POWER WAS ARCO, IDAHO.

THE NAME FITS: AT ALMOST 8,000 FEET DEEP, HELLS CANYON IS THE DEEPEST RIVER GORGE IN NORTH AMERICA.

IN POCATELLO, IDAHO, IT'S ILLEGAL NOT TO SMILE IN PUBLIC. THE LAW WAS PASSED IN 1948 TO TRY TO CHEER PEOPLE UP AFTER A BAD WINTER.

Lewis and Clark thank Idaho for...

We thank Idaho for...

Sacagawea, a Shoshone woman who acted as their interpreter and guide as they explored the West.

television. Philo Farnsworth invented the first television tube in his high school chemistry class in Idaho! (He was born in Utah, though.)

MONTANA COMES FROM THE SPANISH WORD FOR "MOUNTAIN."

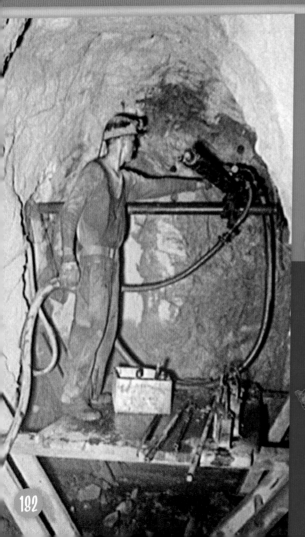

Gold, silver, and lots of copper have all been found in the "Treasure State."

Between 1880 and the early 1990s, Butte, Montana, produced 20.8 billion pounds of copper.

MORE **DINOSAUR EGGS** AND BABY-DINOSAUR SKELETONS HAVE BEEN FOUND IN MONTANA'S EGG MOUNTAIN THAN ANYWHERE ELSE IN THE WESTERN HEMISPHERE.

Custer's Last Stand: The biggest battle in the American Indian Wars took place in Montana in 1876.

WORLD'S SHORTEST RIVER: MONTANA'S 200-FOOT-LONG ROE RIVER. IT'S SHORTER THAN A FOOTBALL FIELD!

Montana is home to more species of mammals than any other state.

THANK MONTANA FOR . . .

BISON CONSERVATION. TEDDY ROOSEVELT ESTABLISHED THE NATIONAL BISON RANGE HERE IN 1908 TO HELP SAVE THE ENDANGERED ANIMAL. IN 2016, PRESIDENT OBAMA MADE THE BISON THE NATIONAL ANIMAL OF THE US.

Nevada

SILVER STATE

MINING ON THE COMSTOCK

Drawn by T.L. DAWES, 1876 — Copyrighted 1877
PUBLISHED BY
J.B. MARSHALL, GOLD HILL, NEV.

Between 1876 and 1878, Nevada's Comstock Lode deposit produced $36 million worth of silver each year.

MORE THAN 200 MILLION YEARS AGO, NEVADA WAS COVERED BY AN OCEAN. FOSSILS OF OCEAN CREATURES CAN STILL BE FOUND IN ITS DESERT.

Nevada's Hoover Dam is, at its base, as thick as two football fields end to end.

Electricity generated at the Hoover Dam serves 1.3 million people in Nevada, Arizona, and California.

WARNING

Restricted Area
It is unlawful to enter this area without permission of the Installation Commander.

While on this Installation all personnel and the property under their control are subject to search.

Use of deadly force authorized.

WARNING!
NO TRESPASSING
AUTHORITY N.R.S. 207-200
MAXIMUM PUNISHMENT: $1000 FINE
SIX MONTHS IMPRISONMENT
OR BOTH
STRICTLY ENFORCED

PHOTOGRAPHY
OF THIS AREA
IS PROHIBITED

WARNING
MILITARY INSTALLATION

IT IS UNLAWFUL TO ENTER THIS INSTALLATION WITHOUT
THE WRITTEN PERMISSION OF THE INSTALLATION COMMANDER

INSTALLATION COMMANDER
AUTHORITY: Internal Security Act, 50
U.S.C. 797
PUNISHMENT: Up to one year imprisonment
and $5,000 fine.

THE FEDERAL GOVERNMENT OWNS MORE THAN 80% OF THE LAND IN NEVADA.

Area 51 is a top secret US Air Force facility in the Nevada desert. Some people believe that crashed UFOs—and the bodies of aliens—are kept there.

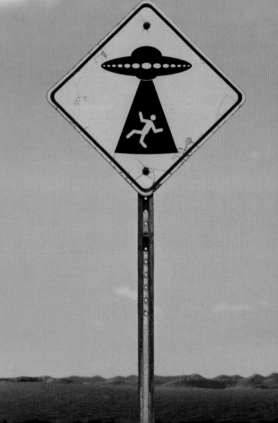

THANK NEVADA FOR . . .

BRIGHT LIGHTS. LAS VEGAS IS FULL OF NEON SIGNS. "VEGAS VIC" IS THE LARGEST NEON MECHANICAL SIGN IN THE COUNTRY.

Oregon

BEAVER STATE

BETWEEN 1841 AND 1884, THOUSANDS OF SETTLERS CAME HERE VIA THE OREGON TRAIL.

Beavers were hunted almost to extinction in the mid-1800s, but the population is flourishing in Oregon again.

LEWIS AND CLARK PASSED THROUGH WHAT IS NOW OREGON ON THEIR WAY TO THE PACIFIC OCEAN. THEY USED THIS COMPASS ON THE EXPEDITION, WHICH LEWIS HAD BOUGHT FOR $5.

Oregon has more ghost towns than any other state.

Crater Lake is the deepest lake in the United States. New York's Empire State Building could be submerged in its watery 1,943-foot depth.

The Humongous Fungus in Oregon's Malheur National Forest is the world's largest known single living organism. It is about 2,400 years old and covers 3.4 square miles.

THE OREGON VORTEX IS A SPOT WHERE BALLS ROLL UPHILL, BROOMS STAND ON END, AND TREES GROW LIKE CORKSCREWS.

THANK OREGON FOR . . .

CHOCOLATE-HAZELNUT SPREAD. THIS STATE GROWS MORE HAZELNUTS THAN ANY OTHER.

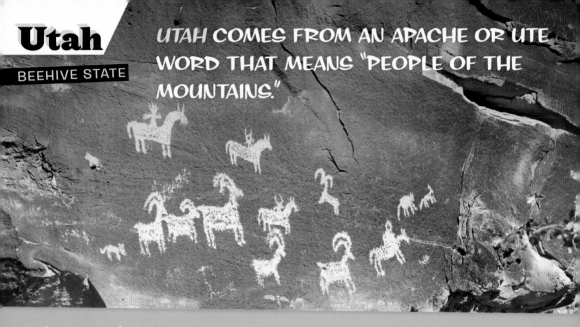

Utah

BEEHIVE STATE

UTAH COMES FROM AN APACHE OR UTE WORD THAT MEANS "PEOPLE OF THE MOUNTAINS."

60% of Utah residents belong to the Mormon Church.

The Mormon Church runs the Family History Library, the largest genealogical research center in the world.

TO THE PEOPLE OF UTAH, THE BEEHIVE WAS A SYMBOL OF THE HARD-WORKING PIONEERS.

In 1869, the US government pressured the Union and Pacific railroad companies to connect. They did so in Promontory Summit, Utah, where there is a replica of the "meeting of the engines."

THE STATE IS ALSO CALLED THE "ROOFTOP OF THE UNITED STATES." IT HAS THE HIGHEST AVERAGE ELEVATIONS IN THE NATION.

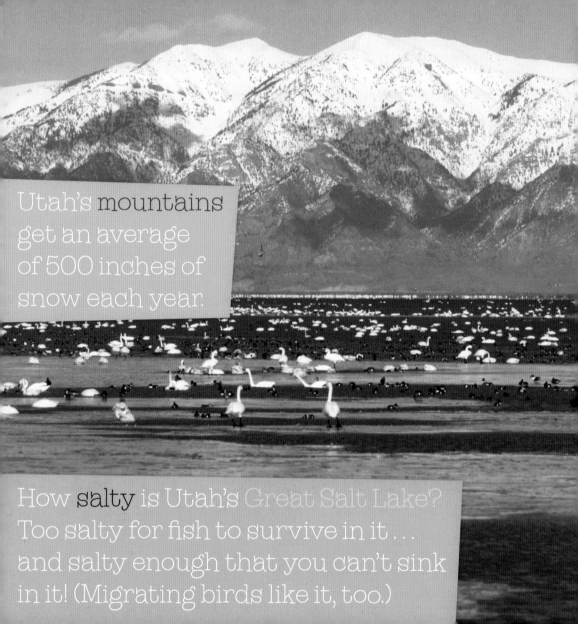

Utah's mountains get an average of 500 inches of snow each year.

How salty is Utah's Great Salt Lake? Too salty for fish to survive in it... and salty enough that you can't sink in it! (Migrating birds like it, too.)

Astronauts use it as a marker when they orbit North America.

Great Salt Lake

THANK UTAH FOR . . .

THE ARTIFICIAL HEART, INVENTED AT THE UNIVERSITY OF UTAH AND FIRST IMPLANTED BY DR. ROBERT JARVIK IN 1982.

EVERGREEN STATE

WASHINGTON IS THE ONLY STATE NAMED AFTER A US PRESIDENT.

ONE-HALF OF THE "EVERGREEN STATE" IS COVERED WITH FORESTS.

The Seattle Space Needle has 25 lightning rods on top to protect it from lightning strikes.

In 1700, an earthquake hit Washington, causing a tsunami so powerful that it also hit Japan.

At 14,416 feet, Mount Rainier is the highest peak in the continental United States. It is an active volcano and last erupted in 1894.

Nearby Mount St. Helens blew its stack more recently: May 18, 1980.

THANK WASHINGTON FOR . . .

FATHER'S DAY! A SPOKANE RESIDENT STARTED THIS HOLIDAY IN 1910 TO HONOR HER DAD, A SINGLE PARENT WHO RAISED SIX KIDS.

APPLES! WASHINGTON GROWS MORE APPLES THAN ANY OTHER STATE.

Wyoming

EQUALITY STATE

VOTES FOR WOMEN

Wyoming was the first state to grant women complete voting rights (1869).

Only about 585,000 people live in Wyoming—fewer than in any other state.

Devil's Tower was America's first national monument.

Scenic ~ WYOMING ~ Folder

POSTAGE
1½ ¢
WITHOUT
MESSAGE

Devil's Tower

America's first national park, Yellowstone, has an official address in Wyoming, but parts of it are in Idaho and Montana.

Yellowstone has 300 active geysers—hot springs that send up tall columns of water and steam.

The Old Faithful geyser erupts every 60 to 110 minutes.

Both Rhode Island and Delaware could fit inside Yellowstone's 3,500 square miles.

THANK WYOMING FOR . . .

COAL. MORE COAL IS PRODUCED HERE THAN IN ANY OTHER STATE.

Washington, DC

Washington, DC, is not a state. It's the capital of the United States.

George Washington chose the capital city's site, which was midway between the northern and southern 13 states.

Washington, DC, gets 39 inches of rain each year—more than drizzly Seattle, Washington!

You can find about 1,800 animals from 300 different species in DC, thanks to the Smithsonian's National Zoo.

Some of DC's most important sites include the White House, the Capitol Building, the Washington Monument, the Lincoln Memorial, the National Mall, the Library of Congress, and the Smithsonian's many museums.

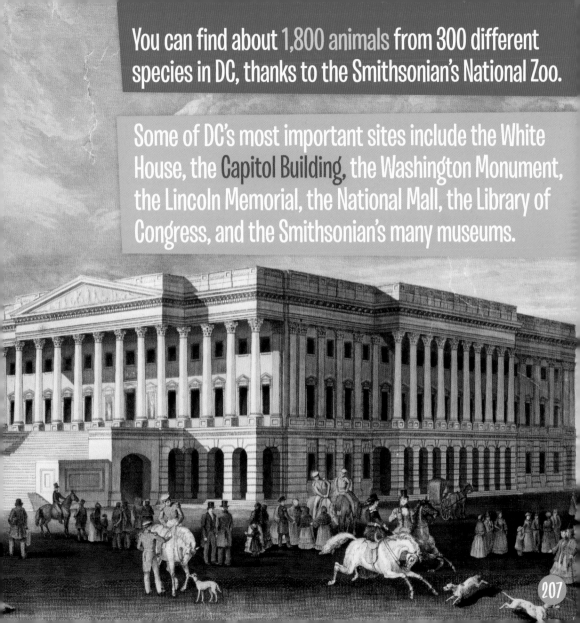